salmonpoetry

Publishing Irish & International

Poetry Since 1981

Ghostlight

New & Selected Poems

Mark Granier

Published in 2017 by
Salmon Poetry
Cliffs of Moher, County Clare, Ireland
Website: www.salmonpoetry.com
Email: info@salmonpoetry.com

ISBN 978-1-910669-91-4

COVER PHOTOGRAPHY: *Mark Granier*
COVER DESIGN & TYPESETTING: *Siobhán Hutson*
Printed in Ireland by Sprint Print

Salmon Poetry gratefully acknowledges the support of
The Arts Council / An Chomhairle Ealaoín

For my father,
in neither memory
nor forgetfulness.

Acknowledgements

Acknowledgements are due to the following print and online publications, where a number of the following poems, or versions of them, first appeared: *The Irish Times, Dublin Review of Books, Southword, The High Window, The Stony Thursday Book, 'And Other Poems', Crannóg, Anthony Wilson's Blog, Headstuff, Daily Poem* and *The New Statesman*.

Some of these poems also appeared in the following anthologies: *World English Poetry*: edited by Sudeep Sen (Bengal Publications, India, 2015), *Fermata: An Anthology of Writings Inspired by Music* (Artisan House, 2016), *The Deep Heart's Core: Irish Poets Revisit Their Touchstone Poems* (Dedalus, 2016).

I am immensely grateful to the Trustees of the estate of Katherine Kavanagh for awarding me a Patrick and Katherine Kavanagh Fellowship in 2016. My special thanks also to Seán Lysaght (again) for his close-reading and helpful suggestions, Johnny Hughes and, especially, Liam Ó Muirthile for his generous introduction, the title, 'Ghostlight', and the delightful pun in the third poem in the sequence, 'Departures.'

Contents

NEW POEMS

Listen hard enough and you wake the dead.

The Slow Shift of Light

Introduction by Liam Ó Muirthile

Mark Granier is a meditative observer, offering us moments of suffused, painterly stillness. In his work there is no undue clamour to be heard, no flashy flailing about in order to be noticed. This might seem to be diffidence, but I perceive it as *integritas*.

He is resolutely detached, has wit, is visually acute, verbally precise, finely tuned and formally in control. Yet you can *feel* his keen mind at work. If, at times, you might wish he cut loose from his moorings and let the rage rage — he does almost take off in 'How Far is Outer Space?' — the poems at all times hold you within their frame. There are very few lyrics in this collection which do not leave a memorable phrase or line, at least, in their trail. As in the early poem 'A Comet At 4 a.m.':

> a flared
> slightly bigger star
> plunging but held

These phrases and lines, a sort of recalling card, invite us to further ponder a poem's afterlife, its implications. When we do so, we come to understand an integrated wholeness in the work, and even a revealing correspondence in our own selves.

I came to Mark Granier's work through *Haunt* which is his pivotal, mature collection, and here amply represented. I remarked: "Although we have the title poem *Haunt* for the grandfather, the "man of the house", the central question, the trope of the whole collection is in the line: "Is a ghost any less a ghost if it's a dream?" I was struck by the recurrence of ghosts, of air in different guises throughout the collection. Mark Granier might say that in *Haunt* he's seeking to make the strange familiar, or at least to familiarise us with what's strange. Now, in the overall context of *Ghostlight: New and Selected Poems*, the missing half of that trope above is in the title. What is remarkable, from very early in the work, is how 'light' in its myriad forms and guises, even in its evanescence, is the underlying theme of many fine poems in the collection. In a sense, the poems seek to embody light, to give it physical form — "a dressing and undressing of light" ('Evening Sun, Bullock Harbour'). Mark Granier may have been a landscape painter in another life.

A poem, too, is the embodiment of sound, that is the intellect harnessed by the musical thrust of the poem, that particular bodily energy of poetry. Mark's marvellous poem 'Vulture Bone Flute — 38,000 BC' — is still one of my favourites from the entire collection and addresses this music full on:

> music that runs like sap
> back to the root
>
> of our species jogging on the spot
> wired to an iPhone — chants, field hollers,
> deafening wars, silences — the body
>
> bearing the mind away
> with riffs, keys, tones, variations
> on what's in us and what will come
>
> to blow through our bones.

'From Blackrock' is a crucial poem which underpins the whole work. I must quote it entire:

> Here's to you, ghost father, alive or dead,
> your surname's reserved seat, your vast
> library of the unsaid;
> to your one image, slip of the past
>
> in blurred grey and white;
> a soldier, sitting with my mother,
> your smile sleepy, hers bright
> as the ghostlight blowing your cover;

to the curse or gift you bestow:
abstraction, my soft spot for absences;
cloudwatcher, seawatcher, open to the slow
shift of light, the wave's always present tenses;

to the given, darkening, Dublin Bay almost black
except, nearby, where a wave splits a rock.

Swamped in a culture inured to subtlety and understatement, it is almost a relief to experience real heartbreak, restored to humanity by a breaking wave.

All good poems are both experiential and aspirational. They are never entirely complete, in the sense that they are always becoming the next poem in some shape or form. It seems to me that "the slow shift of light" is Mark Granier's entry point to a whole range of other poems. His essential theme has found him. His *own* cover is blown. His closing image in 'From Blackrock' becomes his way of finishing other poems — 'Grip Stick', for example:

while I am
abruptly in a different country — the vast
landscape of her open palm —

tiny in the grip of what gave way.

If there is what I call a 'Dublin sensibility', it is well-grounded in *Ghostlight: New and Selected Poems*. I'm particularly fond of 'Fruit Machine' — I love the reference to Pierre's Pool Hall — and of 'Lines For The Diceman' (i.m. Thom McGinty), embedding the visual in the verbal melée of Grafton Street:

a walking painting say, holding its own
gilded ornate frame, the face
white as a mask, Mona Lisa
in a black cat-suit, cracking a murky smile.

The 'Rockville' poems are suburban, interior designs where more than clothes are aired. As a Cork city man and Irish-language writer, I feel, after many years in Dublin, that the city has drifted further across the Irish Sea towards Liverpool and Manchester. Conversely, I myself have drifted further downwind towards France and Spain. Ireland is, after all, a windy isle, easily blown off course. It is always of interest to me from a distance, therefore, how the 'other Ireland' gets a look in. Inis Mór in the Aran Islands features in 'Holding Pattern, Dún Aengus': '...you relish the whole island tilting / its dark-grey wing.' Derrynane graveyard is here and, in 'Bullseye', Spiddal with its rooks' 'cries / sharp as springs bursting from the sky's mattress.'

We catch a glimpse of the eponymous blackbird of Belfast Lough, his "bright-yellow whistle", and there are some versions of Old Irish poems, including the closing poem in the collection, 'How To Ask For A House In Poetry', based on an example in a legal tract of how to request a gift, from Gerard Murphy's *Early Irish Lyrics*. Of most interest to me, however, is the fine poem 'Ringsend' with the epigraph "The Gaelic language was prohibited along with Gaelic dress — saffron-dyed clothing, moustaches, long hair and forelocks", from John O'Beirne Ranelagh's *A Short History of Ireland*.

Besides being a well-trodden path of my own, and a favourite dock-land cityscape, 'Ringsend' successfully subsumes a short poem ascribed to Colmcille — 'Fil súil nglais' (or 'A Blue Eye Will Look Back' in Gerard Murphy's translation) —:

> while a Sealink ferry slides out
> past the Pigeon House, landmark
> chimneys ringed red & white,
> steamship funnels, making of the land an ark
>
> with washing hung on a high-
> security fence (her blouse the forbidden saffron) —
> what a grey or blue or green or brown eye,
> departing, will look back on.

This is, perhaps, as much as us intimates of the Irish language may hope for as a presence in the general scheme of things.

On the other hand, there is much of the English Literary tradition in Mark Granier's work, and I can hear Larkin especially grousing away in the background. Kinsella and Mahon too, of course, and many others. But there is a gentleness, a crooning, in Mark Granier's tone — in his intimate poems for his son and in the mother poems — which is entirely his own: "Total eclipse: you can see the corona's / wild ungovernable curls." ('Hairpin')

It's interesting to note the growing away from earlier poems, which nevertheless carry familiar resonances. For instance,

> not so much 'was
> I here?' as the felt moment's swift
> migration to molecules, its wingbeat
>
> signature in the air —
>
> ('It Isn't Déja Vu')

recalls those great lines in 'Glide-Paths', the first poem in the collection:

> uncoveted wingspan of composure, coming out of nowhere
> to open and air and give you back to yourself.

The "phantom wound" of the new poem is there, after all, despite the once momentary composure and the now molecular affirmation. Many of the poems of *Ghostlight* have lift-off, even a ghostlift-off. Our only wish for Mark Granier is a greater risk-taking, a more brazen and playful formal eruption. He has played his dealt card well and deftly. He has built a solid and enduring body of work on ghostly foundations. As he has built 'How To Ask For A House In Poetry' on a fragment of Old Irish:

> I ask for a house wakeful
> as the cat that also sleeps tight;
> whose opening windows and doors
> breathe like gills, easily exhaling the hard
> feelings, a house that is ready
> as any house can be for catastrophe and delight.

It's fitting that the last word should be delight.

from

Airborne

(2001)

Glide–Paths

Here, high on the sea-looking
east side of Killiney Hill at evening,
you can settle into the glide and reach of space —

a glossed world of sea
swaying inwards behind the hill's shoulder
to smoky towns and mountains low as dunes —

and after a while, sitting
on a granite boulder bedded above the tumbling
scrub of gorse, heather, bramble, nettles, you feel

the uncoveted, fantastic
wingspan of composure coming out of nowhere
to open and air and give you back to yourself.

This, take it or leave it,
is peace, creation going about its business
of recreation, in which one merely and wonderfully

figures, like the white sail-fins
or, precise and patient in the darkening gorse,
spiders weighing the last light, threading the spaces.

A Comet At 4 a.m.

One late last look
before bed, and there
it is, finally, a flared
slightly bigger star
plunging but held,
dissolving in the bluey dark
above sleep-shut houses and gardens.
Brightest on April the first,
the day before I turn forty.
Birthday candle, fuse-light,
your failing exclamation mark
will work its way
to the back of the mind,
where I've let in these words, minutes
tailing from the earthly core
of a spring morning, here
on the doorstep.

Hale-Bopp, Dublin, March 1997

When

When the sky comes down to earth too soon
and we're woven into light's immaculate shroud;
when the black light seeding all our bad dreams blooms
in a spine of smoke bearing aloft the brain-cloud;

when one dies and in that breath millions more
are furnace-fanned to ashes that will blow
wherever the winds rage, burned-out spores
settling, out of the fuming skies, like snow;

when all those seeking Heaven's draughty halls
find the conflagration had to spread,
that angels with singed wings have fled their stalls,
leaving behind the dead to count the dead,

clouds will roll back, a full moon mirror waste
and time do what it always does: erase.

Girl In A Wheelchair Dancing To U2 In Lansdowne Stadium Dublin 1997

In a clearing near midfield
she is tossing her hair, waving her arms,

catching hold of, taking for a wild spin
a new constellation, The Chariot.

The centre holds. Big wheels rattle and hum.
Sparks fly from her.

Holding Pattern, Dún Aengus

At the edge, safe on your belly,
you relish the whole island tilting

its dark grey wing. Below you
seabirds patrolling their levels,

above you a lichen-bright butterfly
haloing crookedly. Your face

is washed by those updrafts, the breath
of a marbling sea. Hang in there

shaken free
at ease in the swim of air.

7Up, Torremolinos

The icy fizz numbs my tongue.
Curving far out, a star-bright
arc-weld of beach on a calm
black sea. The universe is utterly
beyond me, but close. Close.

Seascape In Clare

i.m. Mary Belferman

A perfect day for it, rain
shadowed the coast for miles.
The islands were upturned currachs.

We ordered oysters and they came
arranged for their own funeral.
We scraped out the frilly half-shells

and cupped a slick taste, briny
as the sea made flesh,
sloshed down with a hard white wine.

For the eyes as much as the mouth,
each one a nacreous bloom, a cool bed
peeled back to the sheets.

In Derrynane Graveyard

The roofless chapel holds
stillness in the swirl
of dunegrass and hard rain.

Glass long gone, three slots
distil unaltered light,
a trinity of measures

being taken: unbroken
core samples of sea,
headland and sky.

The Liffey Swim

Nobody creates. The artist assembles memories.

—— Jack B. Yeats

When I found a space between the watchers
on O'Connell Bridge,
the blue wind flapped in my face.

Almost lost in the incoming whitegold, legions
of delicate dark arms
were lifting like timelapse seedlings

and falling like scissors. The old stuff
of tall-storied windows and traffic

banked to each side, new strokes,
a broad afternoon in ribbons.

Ancient View Of Amsterdam

— an etching by Rembrandt

A skyline accumulates from scratch.

Holding under all that air
for the imminent cry of a seagull:

ghost-roofs, ghost-masts —
the hint of a harbour —

then the taller flyweight X
of a windmill, and further off

in the dismantling haze,
three others, lighter and lighter,

cartwheeling across the horizon.

Patchouli

Long-skirted muskiness, trailing a warm breath
of Asia through cool-headed Dublin —
essential oil, a viscous resiny darkness,
dark as distilled cannabis.
You didn't wear it, it wore you, filling your clothes,
even whatever you touched —
glasses, somebody's sheepskin jacket, each other.
A disguise for dope-smokers, they said.
More like a signal, I followed the spoor through dancehalls
and wild Deep Purple weekends.
It was all those warm, warm women I may have met
who reclined on their couches, murmuring
to come in from the cold, to sit, sit over here.

Lines For The Diceman

i.m. Thom McGinty

Good to know you might turn up
in the frieze of faces on Grafton Street,
familiar stranger surprising us
in something from your wardrobe-gallery,

a walking painting say, holding its own
gilded ornate frame, the face
a white mask, Mona Lisa
in a black cat-suit, cracking a murky smile.

Dead-slow, solemnly careful
among eddies of Christmas shoppers, summer dawdlers,
tourists, street-traders, Guards…
mindful of each sound-proofed step, sure-

footed as an acrobat, spaced in, treading your own
high wire. When we looked
at you looking through us
we took in the joke that jumped — a spark of silence —

eye to eye, mind to mind,
across Grafton Street's canyon of swirling clockwork noise.
You're gone now forever (back
into the box with Jack)

and scanning the quickslow, giddy, sedate
everyday street-portrait — its procession
of invisible masks — the eye misses you.
Old Master, Diceman, conductor

of the ungrooved thought, catcher
of the thrown glance, are you still there?

from

The Sky Road

(2007)

Before And After

for Samantha and Simon

1

Watching sea and sky
darken and simplify,

I think of what's now in hand —
the stubby, white plastic wand

you drew from your handbag to show
(in its recessed, thumbnail window)

two, clear-blue lines,
one light, one darkly defined:

a skipped heartbeat, a stone
out of sight, over the known

peaceable old horizon
I had rested my eyes on.

*

Now he is sounded, swept
into webbings of light,

restless, more and less real,
metaphors on a roll,

none clearer than the top
of his skull: oval, a raindrop

let go, falling on course,
eye to eye with the Earth

dreaming up sun, moon, stars
in its hammock of waters.

2

Stroking his forehead, I found it
by accident, that soft spot
under the skin, where the young bone
knits... knits... knits...

His lopsided, premature smile
is a quiver of pain. He is all
there, solid, a touchstone
in touch, *a part of the main*.

3

This is how I find he has nosed
his spreading taproot down
into my days.
                          I come to
in my old pose, at a window,
lightly swaying from foot
to foot,
              as if nursing more
than a paperback (his warm bulk);
surprised to find our rock-
abye rhythm — the day itself,
                                    gentled,
cradling my old head —
even in prose.

Boy

He was a real boy,
with a high, bony forehead

and hair I'd have called mousy
if I'd known the word;

pleading eyes, blue-grey skin
that never looked warm:

stalk-necked, a fledgling
shivering in the icy spotlight

where words die.

*

Once, at my bus stop,
he approached me shyly

and offered me a Dinky 'if
you'll be my friend.'

As soon as I took it I saw
I must give it back

before catching my bus home
where I knew I was loved.

*

One day, he wasn't there,
along with that airless distance

I could have bridged with a look.
I can't remember when I felt

his absence, or came awake
to how lonely it is.

Footholds

Somewhere down there, underfoot,
there are oak woods stuffy with silence
and airbrushed with its variations: hisses, creaks,
cricks, whiffles, rustles, a flurry of sighs...
the whole island detached, nestling, adrift
and at home in its own sea.
A solitary cuckoo, then a blackbird's bright-yellow whistle
illuminates the air. No one has a hand in this
outfitting, rust-dark, sap-green, accumulating
wing upon wing, fan upon fan, a map
of smells for the pygmy shrew. Everything
tickles itself with its own brilliance, weighs
in with the same gravity. Warming mountains. Cloud-
shadows broader than mountains. A beetle
flashing its shield. Sticks. Stones.
Babel-towers
of untoppled, sky-scraping *shhh*.

                    *

Something has struck, the faint muffled *thock*
of stone on bark. A new time. A new clock.

                    *

On calm days we take stock, thank the old flatfaced sea
for pretending to sleep sound. Inland the woods thicken
with inquisitorial shadows. Out of nowhere the sky
slams shut a black trapdoor. Something is loose
up there. Boulders as big as the world roll
over the world. Lightning violates the air
indelibly. Then up comes the next day's ache
of fathomless blue, bog-cotton clouds. No need
for the written word. Above our heads the gods
we've found names for mingle with those we don't know.
The softheaded mountains speak.

From Blackrock

Here's to you, ghost father, alive or dead,
your surname's reserved seat, your vast
library of the unsaid;
to your one image, slip of the past

in blurred grey and white —
a soldier, sitting with my mother,
your smile sleepy, hers bright
as the ghostlight blowing your cover —

to the curse or gift you bestow:
abstraction, my soft spot for absences;
cloudwatcher, seawatcher, open to the slow
shift of light, the waves' always present tenses;

to the given, darkening, Dublin Bay almost black
except, nearby, where a wave splits a rock.

Western Stills

for Johnny Hughes

Moon On Inis Mór

There's a chink in the rolling cloud-wall, glint
of stone light on stone fields, this
sliding moment.

Approaching Dún Aengus

Wave-thunder — the whole
island's a tall house; downstairs
the sea's at the door.

Indreabhán, 5 a.m.

Steepling behind your
house on the hill,
the vertical, bone-white oar
of a windmill.

On The N6

Thin, tall, armless, a thawing ghost
of a snowman — a milestone
for where miles go.

Lightbox

(Newgrange)

Everyone should have one
dark hub for the dull day's orbit:

stoneshouldered wings
where you bury the bones

of belief, and the redfaced sun,
to gain entrance, turns

a skeleton key.

The Box

Sucks, but is beautiful.
I was raised in its milky light, fell
for The Man From U.N.C.L.E., Astroboy, Dr Who.

Thought-proofing for the old winged chariot's out-of-the-blue-
doom on our doorstep. Nothing
is new after all:

pristine, natural
as any surfacing thought-bubble, the wheel
pinwheeling in our eyes millennia before the dream

of cartwheels, sputtering rotors spun to a gleam.
Feeler to the stars, the bottom-silt
dark where they dwell

down the telescope-well;
our unfledged, twitchy buzz pulsed
far from the watery cloudnest. When you flick

it off, brush from the dark screen those webs of static,
inevitable in the primeval smog is this
square egg, warm still.

Find

for Joe Woods

No modern paving-brick, this
lopsided ovoid, raw
stone drawn from the mud

of a cobbled, medieval Drogheda.
Unshaped and shapely
as a handy wedge, touchstone

nestled in a dry-stone wall.
But here is one corner rubbed
smoother and darker, netted

with feathery scratches: off-centred
diamond eye, taste-bud,
tiny dint in the soundtrack

of dog paws, cattle hooves, slap
of bare feet, sandals (or soles
of whatever passed for shoes),

clatter of iron rims, hush
of snow, and the rain's hiss
metalling sun- or moonlight.

In my hand now's a gift
I can hold and heft, sniff
for the never far-off sea,

bump it gently against
my skull — stone to bone — even
kiss it, try one new

note on the old scale,
the rattling run of a town
given its day in the sun.

Fruit Machine

Pierre's Pool Hall on Stephen's Green. Bored with pool,
table-soccer, screeching cars, I slotted 50p, watched
the prayer-wheel spin — lemons, cherries, black bars —

till it jammed on three melons, trembled slightly and spewed
£80, more than a week's wages then,
as if a whole silvery orchard shook itself

and stood still, a drench of what seemed like actual luck;
till Friday, back on a bee-line, thinking *screw it*,
a little loose change from the wage packet...

They are offered, sweet plunges, gear sticks to crest the high
shifting dunes, juicy mirages we won't reach or even
want to, the aftertaste a mouthful of old coins;

like the frosty night I sped down Killiney Hill,
took a sharp corner, for a freeze-framed eye-blink, hit
black ice, the steering wheel spinning, a useless toy —

lemons, cherries, black bars, a trance, a trip
through a hole in the world — gripping just in time
to swerve from the wall.

From Mount Street Bridge

That night three girls were swimming there
between the tall reeds

in the canal, bare arms and legs waving
palely in the dark water;

laughing, shaking their hair, tossing
an affectionate 'fuck off'

to someone standing on the bank. We loitered
to breathe it in: soft skin

and loud voices, ambering in the dark water,
close to the road, the streetlights.

For Dust

Sleepless on my mother's bed, in the tall
room of our Bournemouth hotel (outside,
red squirrels in the dim pines)
I listened, for the first time,
to my own mystifying heartbeat,
a word, a word in my ear
I could not decipher. Squirrels,
auburn flames, darted, flickered,

flared into a dark road, headlit,
a child in the passenger-seat
startled by a fox, a dusk streak —
one of those passwords for passing —
finely sharpened, vanishing
into the ash-cloud of its tail.

Here, There

for Isobel Stephenson

Raised in Dublin, your home-heavy bones ached
for flight, a skimmed ocean, a bed
in some high-vaulted city, vined with neon, the bee dance
of headlights and tail lights, any place
the levelling mind is lulled in its drift towards sleep
by tunings, notes in a new key,
whirl of a foreign siren, scream
of laughter in a different language.

You fell in love with (and in) San Francisco,
purled up the Mekong Delta,
trekked through a few of those scuffed,
uncluttered zones on the atlas — a clearing
on a thick-wooded hillside where you felt,
quaking the Mongolian earth,
a quickening thunder rolling to burst from the trees —
a flare of wild horses, earthcoloured, spurred
by the ghosts of Tartars, tails and manes
flowing triumphant.
                                If,
in some unimaginable future
your feet finally stop beating their wings
and the 'survived by' dare to bury you here
in Dublin, they'll feel a breeze palping their cheeks,
in their shoes a shifty dust-angel
curling the toes, in their ears a little whorl-wind
of possibility:
                    Look, my home's in the air
ringed more than once with my flight-paths,
before it's too late now crawl
out of the hard shell of your birthplace, take
my hand — a sinew of wind — and leave only one word
graved for the rain to blur: Elsewhere

The Golden Gate:
Crossing The Chord

'…I instantly realized that everything in my life
that I'd thought was unfixable was
totally fixable — except for
having just jumped.'

A Blessed Curse

for the Human Race

May your children and your children's children
marry, again, and again, he or she whose skin
is unmistakably (even in a dim light) that shade
that has you most affronted and afraid,
and may these marriages be
devastatingly happy.

Portraits Of A Grouse-Beater, 1975

Your line advances over the Colonel's moor,
to scare up a drumming of wings (go Back! go Back!)
and wave them towards the expensive tweed, the dogs.

                *

Lunch with other beaters: sandwiches, beer.
Reaching for a can of Tennants, see your hand
close over the girl on the can, *Heather*, in pink.

                *

But you came to find the hard-paying, hard-hatted work.
A roustabout on the rigs. A roust-a-what?
Something to do with chains that can rip an arm off.

                *

In the cockpit of the jeep with the Yorkshire ex-Angel.
His grown-up tash and sideburns. He flips his lighter
and a sleepy moth goes up, then down in flames.

                *

Barely aware of the signals you send out.
The Glasgow bootboy (tidy and short, tats
on his Popeye forearms) refuses to meet your eyes.

                *

Laughing, he 'accidentally' spills his whiskey
on your grimy jeans. So, laughing, you pour yours
into his lap, his knife-creased Oxford Bags.

                *

Your poems and drawings: doodles in the margins
of doodles, a diary of loose ends. The marginal god
of fools, drunks and dossers watches over you.

                *

He is up before you can blink, head-butting, thrashing,
screams, as they drag him off and hold him back,
he'll take you on bare-handed: '...you can have the axe!'

     *

A cooling hearth. Glasgow has gone to bed,
and the others, except for the biker who quietly begins
to try to explain exactly how worthless you are.

     *

You keep schtum. What is he trying to push you towards?
Self-knowledge? Suicide? You can always use
more of the first, travelling far too light.

     *

So dreamy you never figured to sign on
in Edinburgh — somewhere to bring a girl,
breathe on a bedsit pane, patch out the world.

     *

Found in the heather: the bleached skull of a mouse,
a brown-red feather, a dirty tuft of wool —
sewn to your army jacket like a badge.

The Circuit

Oh ring, ring, open wide and let us out! —
Anne Frank

1. ANNE FRANK'S HOUSE

From the blacked-out upper windows we can see
the gauzy 1940s, a barge parked
in a neat canal, a girl going past on a bicycle.

Walls no longer hold their breath, they talk,
flickering on each cleared-out floor, a further part
of the looped story, while the tourist file unwinds
to wander the dim levels.
                              Where I can find
no trace of the irrepressible being whose kiss
would crumple the walls, send ripples, sparks, connections
down traintracks, shivery lines of canal water.

2. THE RIJKSMUSEUM: REMBRANDT SELF PORTRAIT

She has joined us after all, darkhaired, one step
ahead, as we shuffle past and graze with our eyes
the curls' lit filaments, warm burrow of his gaze
tailing us downstairs into the cooling sun.

3. SKATING RINK

Beneath the museum, a walkway, echoing arch
of train-tunnel dimness, then unshuttered day, re-entry.
At the edge of some acres of open grass, an eddy
of swirling laughter and faces. I miss her glance
again, but she'll come round again, her line
woven freehand into those joyous orbits.

4. Van Gogh Museum

Each one a handprint, whorl of a furious decade.
Tall, red leggings, black skirt, grey fleece jacket,
white hair in a short ponytail, she's elegant
and still as a stork, a witness looking in

at apples, lemons, pears, a frothy platter
of ochres, leafgolds airy as blown glass
blazing and brimming its borders to spill and colour
the flat wood frame
                    sky-billowing, open wide
a window for us to fly through, thumbed with light.

Prelude

I wake to find a grey day waiting.
Fog has bulldozed our long
suburban avenue to a blurred
cul-de-sac. Where's the bored hum

of cars in the early rat-run,
brattling magpie or sweet air
of some smaller, unknown bird?
Stillness, a world on mute.

Then it comes, that deep, brassy note
shivering the inner ear,
as it might be the first of a whole
orchestra at sea, tuning up.

So this is what we were waiting for:
more, more...

from

Fade Street

(2010)

Sing, Words

That you may survive
those star-grazed years after I've
gone back to where I'm going: air

of a song, dead air, my dark star
set in the glimmerless hush,
cool enough to touch.

Sing, that something remain
of these epic, mundane
conversations hoofing it down my back

clicketty clack —
that you may hit or miss
with a flourish, a backdraught, a hiss

like intaken breath. Life itches to get out
of its mildewed coats,
glint with the motes turning

in a slanted beam — O sing
the slow schoolboy's daydream
counting them in.

A Photograph Of Fade Street, Dublin, 1878

The exposure, half a minute? Enough for light's breath
to cloud the glass with this narrow
Georgian canyon: dark fanlights

above dark doors, sash windows raised
while the far end assumes its name, greys
to a smoky membrane.

Steady as a gramophone needle behind his tripod,
the afternoon swirling about him,
time's pupil concentrates on

the cogs and gears. Three girls perched on a kerb
will be restless smears; two boys
sitting on a doorstep may take

if they keep staring, contracted in the same hard gaze
as their grown ups: two men
in bowlers, huddled on the next

step. Nearer, the pair of women who stand
talking with a third (held sharp
in her street-level window)

sway themselves into ghosts with a pale-faced lad
flickering from a doorway.
Others, too fast, walk

through the boxed walls, empty themselves up steps,
withdraw — an old man tapping the pane
gone, a cat in the railings —

children who whirr, sparrow across the street —

Bicycle Seat
Bull's Head
Bull-Leap

— *Picasso, 1942*

Here's an answer —
slim-skulled, playful, austere,

clear as the nose —
to a problem no one had posed:

how to release the bull
from the bicycle

so handlebar horns offer
a leap, charged with laughter.

The Older Standing Army

Decamped some time ago, rank upon rank,
to the rooftops.

Here they lift pint pots
of evening and morning sun, and perhaps one

in ten brandishes a plant, an antique aerial or
is garlanded with a nest.

Most of them are not
speaking now, pillars of a too high, too clear

society of coos and caws, star-hammered doors,
blue-greys or anaemic

no less exhausted air.
Nevertheless, they are still organs of the snug,

coughing, whiskey-lit, smoke-signalled city, its fug
louring in low clouds.

Who else to uphold
all those burnt columns of births and deaths, the gold

worked into the old lining, the grimecoat?

One Of The Houses
James Joyce Lived In,
Once

for Ak

James Joyce ivy
on James Joyce plaque,
James Joyce pebbles
on James Joyce dash,
James Joyce knocker
on James Joyce door,
James Joyce dust
on James Joyce floor,
James Joyce windows
with James Joyce glass
waiting for James Joyce
clouds to pass.

Night, Wind, Dead Leaves

rattle and hiss, the sound so high
it is almost a whistle,

their bodying sigh
the air of something more palpable

than passing by.

Crest

On a drystone wall a stoat
stops, as if taking

its own pulse: rampant
heraldic stand-in for

the whole family — stone,
earth, water, fire...

fluidly gone,
          so
sky readjusts to sky,

grass to grass,
drystone to dry stone.

There's Probably No God.
Now Stop Worrying
And Enjoy Your Life

—— Ad by The Atheist Bus Campaign

Not only
is there
probably
no god,
but this is
probably
not your bus.

Fruit Bats In Sydney

1. EVENING, PORT ELIZABETH

Four stories up, at the appointed hour,
we watched it begin: a scatter of sooty flakes

rose from the softlit city (an upside down chandelier)
outriders' pterodactyl wings

smuttering, near.

2. AFTERNOON, BOTANIC PARK

On the barer branches clumps
of burn-coloured fruit unhooked to hang-glide

blue gaps. Their shit anointed the paths, a loamy
counterpoint to the bustle and bloom,

invisible caves to step through.

Three Riddles And A Limerick

Sometimes I'm a knife,
sometimes a feather,
sometimes a bulldozer.
Before I came along
trees couldn't find their tongues.
Now the forests are full of whispers.

*

You might be pleased to see me
or find me too honest for words.
But come close, breathe on me
and I'll vanish obediently.

*

It is we who have to bear the weight
of every creature walking the earth.
We are glad only one of these
sees fit to imprison us
in soft coffins,
keeping us in the dark.

*

There once was a boy called Robartes
whose doctor insisted 'No Smarties!
or you'll grow up to perne
in a gyre with Aherne
and the rest of those high-talking hearties.'

Lookout

The lowest branch a bar to help you climb
into the V, then heave through the square hole
in the floor: a nest of plywood, forgotten doors
my cousin banged together one day, for years
cradled in our tallest apple tree. That's me

on the roof's half-rusted, corrugated iron,
standing under the sun, staring away
over neighboring trees, roofs, fields, to make out
Howth Head's cagy embrace, and just below it,
a stubborn flake of ultramarine. I grip

bendy branches: knuckly, sap-green cookers
(too bitter to sink your teeth in, too many to harvest)
and throw my weight from one foot to the other
till the whole shapeless vessel creaks and sways.

The Last Wolf In Ireland

Pray you, no more of this; 'tis like the howling
of Irish wolves against the moon.

                 — As You Like It

Was hunted down, caught and skinned like the others.
Was neither seen nor heard.
Was heard howl one last time, at a slip of a moon
blacked out in cloud.
Was never even rumoured as it skirted the nets
of history and symbol.

Was glimpsed once, fifty years after
all wolves were declared gone —
a lean face a narrow wedge
of paler dusk, between what was left of the oaks —
by a horseman who crossed himself
in fear or reverence or both
and spoke of it to no one.

Was anywhere, nowhere, a face in a folded pack,
a title searching for a poem
facing extinction.

'Don't End With History Or The Sea'

a poet warns us, or you'll make each thing
'sound like everything else.'

Here, above Blackrock, everything slopes
to that great, warped lens.
Buildings stand in the way, borrow the light.

Days, nights, when there is nowhere better to look,
I sometimes drive there, park at a low wall
in Sandycove or Seapoint,
to write or just sit, long enough to take home
equilibrium, one little bucket of history

slopping gently on whatever scales
register these things.

from Departures

Long after the Irish (A.D. 600 — 1200)

COLUM CILLE'S DERRY

Beyond doubt, I love Derry,
so calm, bright and airy —

on each hill, every street,
angels adjusting the light.

THE HOSTING

It is a king's work, this hosting
of all of Adam's seed,
and yet is it no work, nothing
at all, and it proceeds.

No sooner do they know
than they study to forget
where the hosting goes —
no one is ready yet.

When you are called forth,
if you refuse to leave,
in whose house, whose fort
will you stand siege?

PAYMENT IN KINE

He'll never trade you a horse
for a beautiful, thoroughbred verse.

He will offer you something hollow
as his heart: an old cow.

Memo

Remember the hour
when a real foot stands on real earth — it leaves the print
of a centaur,
a whiff of horse-sweat and wild mint.

You might start there.

from

Haunt

(2015)

Grip Stick

The man emptying bins on the prom might be my age,
though healthier looking, tanned, bare-armed
in a hi-vis jacket and black ski-cap.
He plucks at stray bits of litter with that familiar
metal rod with its Dalek pincer — the same

as the one I bought for my mother in Fannin's
some years before she died — a gadget
so starkly ingenious surely it's a branch
of a family tree of similar inventions, of Bakelite,
whalebone, leather, wood… going back, back

to that afternoon in her nursing home
a year and a half ago, when I hold her hand
and feel it loosen then go slack, and call
the nurse, who says quietly 'yes, she's going…'
and I look out the window

to see the usual glorious rubbish, clouds
not stopping their tumble over Killiney Hill's
huddle of slates and satellite dishes, while I am
abruptly in a different country — the vast
landscape of her open palm —

tiny in the grip of what gave way.

Bullseye

Spiddal at dusk, in the rear-view a grainy swirl
over the rooftops — starlings? — that murmuration
I'd hoped to witness. Swerving, pulling in
under the copse near the church, I saw

what it was: rooks, their cries
sharp as springs bursting from the sky's mattress —
a murderous parliament swelling, shrinking, circling
the tattered wind of itself, black

as the trees taking them back,
coming in low so my upturned face felt
the fury, and a single hard tap
on my shoulder could only be

that species of luck, accuracy.

'How Far Is Outer Space?'

If you take a car and aim it
straight up you can arrive in under an hour
without breaking the national speed limit.

But first, you will need to find the right
car, my broken-in, grey-blue 323
with the James Bond pop-up headlights.

Comfortable as a pair of old trousers, those trips
when I pulled hedged-in nightscapes
around me, up to my hips.

No CD or airbag, though you can allow
your airbag mind to inflate, fill every crevice
from the foot-well to the rear window.

Gun the angle, push the stick all the way
into vertical, flick on the high beams
and you're away, a bulging roar

of dust in gravity's layby.

from Academic

CHEMISTRY

The lovely wrongness of mercury.
I ask Paddy where we can get some, so

he asks the Japanese boy, Sato,
who escorts us into the empty lab

as if he owns it. We tip
a whole Aspirin bottle's worth out of a tube

and before we can wonder
what to do with it, Paddy — in secret communion

with some inner double-dare — rolls
one of those molten heavyweight pearls

off his palm onto his tongue.

CONFIRMATION

How difficult can it be?
Transubstantiation? The Trinity?

But when the soft face under the tall hat mouths
'Who made the world?' it wafer-melts

into its echo: the one test
you could not fail to pass, or digest.

LATIN

Mr Banks' drone could not be drier
as he conjugates: amo, amas, amat...
till a terrible drought rolls in along the Tiber,
the flagons empty, love itself gone flat.

FRENCH

Mr Feutren (Fruity) isn't from France
but Brittany. Important. Make no mistake.
Something — anger? passion? — has shorn his face
to a bald, beak-nosed, hunched-electric presence.

Yes, he fought with the SS during the war.
A Breton nationalist, why should he hide
what he believes? What he did was justified
(though I'm not sure who these justifications are for).

The Irish, so *stupide*! Hard to believe
how little we know, and how can we make a start
when, in restaurants, we ignore the hearts
of artichokes, to nibble at the leaves.

Now he has lost patience and swoops to wrench
some slowcoach from his desk. I am in his sights
and will be next. Because of (or despite)
whatever he fled, he teaches excellent French.

A Reading

No matter if you're a dosser or a swot,
when asked to read a poem aloud the protocol
is to sound like a bored robot —

then Kinsella's Garden on the Point
where 'the speckled bean breaks open' and 'the snail
winces and waits', and the brunt

of some odd imperative pushes me ahead
of myself, to brace my elbows, cover my ears
and read it, for once, the way it should be read.

The Catch

Not a team player, even in a team of one,
I could rarely conscript myself
to that sweeping aside, great clear-felling of woes,

though I admired the way the oval ball
got reborn, wobbling out
from a thicket of muddy legs,

or how soccer's untouchable orb — shrunk to a bright
dot on the duplicate screens —
touched like a bolt, brought the lounge to its feet,

and sometimes, channel-surfing,
I fell in with Wimbledon's sharp little grunts and thwacks
that made of the air something

furiously lashed and strung, harp of lines
firm enough to climb
to a kind of music: swing, kick, dance

out of civilised skin, into
instinct and brilliance — worn green oblongs shot through
with jazzy, doodling grace notes, raptures

of disappointment, even their own
concise stretches of boredom boggy and grey
as infinity — yet the lovely

footloose physics of it all
somehow seemed less riveting
than table soccer or slot-machines in Pierre's Pool Hall.

Something in me backed off
from gladiatorial ecstasies, or preferred them
filtered by distance: my high-ceilinged,

mouldy bedsit on Mountjoy suddenly aired
by one of those windy roars — a ball missed
or saved in nearby Croker —

to which I raise a toast: Here's
to the maker of whatever happened or didn't, the catch
in drifts of silence, cheers.

Haunt

Grandfather, you were the man of the house,
the one who slacked the fire and rose at dawn
to poke it into life, a waking pulse.

You hated night-lights burning, would come down
in your stockinged feet, to flick the Bakelite switch:
our whispers in solid dark, abruptly drowned.

So I find myself, back in the old-fashioned kitchen
of the place you bought (and we sold) — a fitting home,
though I was far too absent to know it then.

Sheets on the indoor washing line. I part them
to see the door already swinging open,
the moment closing in, trailing its hem.

Is a ghost any less a ghost if it's a dream?
You're tired, slightly stooped in your wine-red jumper,
grey sides of your bald head slick with Brylcreem.

Our eyes don't meet. I know why we are here:
for you to begin again, retell each story
and me to finally listen, and remember.

I rifle the nearest dresser drawer (the one
with rubber gloves, corks, scissors, snarls of twine...)
for a pencil stub and anything to write on.

You sigh, ask for 'a cup of tea', and I take
those words down as the dream-silt stirs and dims
and muddles me awake.

Planet Y

At five he tells us 'you can choose when you die,
you go to the Dying Spot and jump in.'

Later, going to bed, he has questions
our careful answers cannot begin to satisfy.

So he tells us what he hopes for, a planet where
we wake after we die: its laws

that nobody dies and there is no school 'because
everyone knows everything.'

Some nights, you can almost bring it in focus,
a furiously coloured-in dot

that might be a dead pixel, a flaw in the glass
or might not.

Five Lizards

1. BENIDORM 1966

It could let go its tail if caught.

Fat siesta sun full
on my back, I kept still, held
myself invisible, in love
with its dry archaeological scuttle

quicker than thought.

2. SILVES 2001

Those two, geckos with the magic toes —
guardians of our rented house
in Portugal. While we watched

the terrible loops of data on CNN —
the towers turned
into blooming smoky candles again and again —

they returned each night and set
under the porch light
short delicate shadows.

3. MALAGA 2004

When you threw another log on the fire
something half-fell, half-

scrambled, smoking on the hearth.
Must have been asleep in the woodpile. For

a handful of heartbeats it froze
as if considering — flagstones, open door

to the Andalusian stars —
before skittering back to its bolt-hole, the core

raftered with blue-orange flame —
safe as ashes, as clay,

already part of the same
sky we'd be vapouring into the following day.

4. Inis Mór 2005

Saw a sand lizard's face poke
out of a slice

of blackness in a gryke
and was vouchsafed

something of the island's discrete
micro-climates — time zones

seeded between the old
carboniferous floors,

intimate architectures —
elaborate flying buttress

of bramble and tiny, rare
nova-flowers that burn

in there with feathery tails
of scaly male-fern.

Ringsend

The Gaelic language was prohibited along with Gaelic dress —
saffron-dyed clothing, moustaches, long hair and forelocks.

John O'Beirne Ranelagh, *A Short History of Ireland*

Point of the tide, spit of land, *An Rinn*
where you could stay low and dry
outside the city walls, *sa bhaile*, The Green
Patch where The Dodder and The Liffey

bled into the sea's industry — air
briny and clean off the wrinkled sand or it swings
from the lower circles, sulphur —
end of the moorings, iron rings

threaded with ropes, the crew ashore
drinking at the sign of The Good Woman,
a fanlight intact or gone in above the hall door,
rum, cotton, coffee, tobacco, resin...

the city dump smoothing its dunes
shaken by raucous gulls to a snow-globe
where hand-to-mouth, ragged platoons
stumbled, stooped, probed

for anything, a gleam like a ring in barmbrack,
the recycled riddle
crunching a razor-shell — container ships, stacks
of bibles and ironsides, landfill-

name that reclaims itself, sings, begets
lorries, Travellers, tidal traffic —
from The Salmon Pool to the light on Poolbeg — nets
and net curtains, shipshape village of red brick,

Quality Row, Whiskey Row, drone
of dirt bikes revving near the Waste Water Treatment Plant
buffered by the bird sanctuary's green zone —
a Brent Goose, a wing-stretching cormorant —

ebbing, bay-wide emptiness, the bare scroll
cloud-lit, in a steady state
of arrival, where a solitary soul
with bucket and spade, digging for bait,

pauses, while a Sealink ferry slides out
past the Pigeon House, landmark
chimneys ringed red & white,
steamship funnels, making of the land an ark

with washing hung on a high-
security fence (her blouse the forbidden saffron) —
what a grey or blue or green or brown eye,
departing, will look back on.

Keys

At 18, I wore a bunch of them — pendants
on a leather thong. I wanted secrets

to keep, the jingle, the little teeth
turning the pins, old

tangible symbols. As if I might learn to belong
by playing at being warder

to a makeshift life: the front door
to my first home, Rockville (the only one

with an actual name); the flat
with a fire escape that stopped short

of tousled, fogbound gardens, a neighbour
calling her cat in 1974;

the padlock that released, from Stephen's Green,
one buckled bicycle wheel;

the cardboard and leather suitcase I inherited
from grandfather, who'd kept it

under his bed, perhaps so he could sleep
on old letters, tinted postcards,

a big brass paddle and key
to a hotel room high in The Windy City.

from Rockville

White and blue, simple lines —
the house where I was raised

aged like anyone, grew
a beard of Virginia creeper
whose feelers felt between frames.

Here is a place we might have kept
instead of being haunted by,
that is holding, to this day,

keystones — the air in those rooms.

                *

In the top drawer, so different from
the soft, neatly folded clothes, her necklaces —
pearls and beads, the pink coral —

trickle and click through my fingers, feel
the precise weight of the tangle
of memory and dream.

                *

Cloakroom under the stairs

cools its heels. A waft
from its curtained alcove: old boots,
turps, Brasso, shoe polish,

blue and red lino, a narrow aisle
padded on one side
with the family's gallery of cloaks:

my mother's orange sheepskin
(from *One Million Years B.C.*),

grandfather's weathered mac
and trilby, the cocky, offwhite
golfer's cap (disapproved of),

grandmother's Persian lamb,
her mink stole's tiny paws
and hard-nosed, rodent faces

slow my travelling hand.

*

The heavy-headed roses have grown
dishevelled, swaying above her

as she stoops with secateurs
among upright, woody stems, extravagant thorns,

burying, I once pompously wrote,
'her regret' (At what? Not having lived

a more ordered or wildly-lived life? Not being sure
of herself or what she should do?).

More likely just pleasuring, becoming lost in
velvety pinks, creams, carmines

curling like old photographs
tattered and edged here and there

with tea-brown stains.

*

Grandmother folds her Evening Press and points
at something in Dubliner's Diary, The Gay Sweatshop:
'Mark, who are all these "gay" men? Why
are they so happy?'

*

The green ribbed trunk belonging to my uncles
lives on the landing, part of the house's time

machinery, heady aroma of old books, brass
and leather: a holster, a bullet casing, a tome

on forensic medicine (good for a dose of horror),
an agonised Christ's head carved from Plasticine,

a microscope, a stained-glass smear of blood,
a paperback of Sartre's *Intimacy*...

*

Behind the drawing room,
the dimmer, colder dining room
looks north. Lunch on the table,
palms are steepled: *Bless us*
our Lord for these thy gifts...

Amen. Not much else
is said, unless grandfather
drop-clatters his knife and fork
to storm through the French windows
with his old war cry: 'Get out of it!' —

flapping a great white serviette
at the barely disturbed birds
in the topmost branches, dining
on our apples and pears.

*

I am summoned again, handed
the oil-dark scissors to clip
from behind his purple ears, the silvery eaves.

And again: bright summer evenings,
he sits hunched in the bath while I sponge
his bony, freckled shoulders.

Distances, hard words, words
that should have passed between us
here in the wash of light

through clouded glass, the comforting
faintly sour smell of the facecloth,
each echoey drop

of water on water — skin.

                    *

Removal: a grey day
buries itself briskly. In the coffin:

creased and set, the wax-&-iodine
kernel of his face.
                    Outside, afterwards,
an elderly nun is shaking everyone's hand:
'He was a warrior, he was a warrior...'

Neary's

Half a lifetime since we met for the first
and last time in a crowded pub, our talk,
like the cigarette smoke, layered and dispersed;

like ourselves, lifted on a draft
of faint perfume and pheromones,
into the alley. She mentioned a flight (a path

uncrossed: off my map, east or west or south).
And her number? And if? And when? She sealed
such questions with her silencing mouth.

Nope, I Haven't Yet Figured Out What Beauty Is For

— a response to Mary Oliver

Sure, your wild geese can drag me willy-nilly
with a choked sob into their sky

and I agree that dogs, swans, mockingbirds and doe-eyed stones
deserve to have souls,

but sometimes I want to shout (since a stone can not)
that these have as much need of souls

as the butterfly has of a pin, the biologist's mouse
of the human ear cloned on its back;

that to pile onto furry things spiritual quilts patched
out of wounded rapture

can chill rather than warm, make a soul's teeth chatter
for those others with hardly a stitch:

sea cucumbers, viruses, space junk — the rice grain that fell
from a bird's skull-socket, curled

and writhed in my palm as if butting the swell
of this too-living wall.

High Rise Squat, 1989

A crowbar, that was the thing,
as if I was prising the lid
off a crate, rather than climbing
into a crow's nest for a stowaway.

Across the Channel — the street party
to end all parties — Berlin
was tearing itself together: *Go over and see.*
I kept my head down, stayed in,

fixed a great plastic sheet
in the smashed window: days
that sagged, at peace, or wind, rain, sleet
snapped and rattled my sail.

Found a girlfriend instead of my feet
(so no need to pull up my socks).
Six months, a blink, an age:
skies packing and unpacking while the blocks

stood around us like luggage.

Present Continuous

Going on two months after you're dead
and I am still saying 'good morning mum'
and before closing the door on what was your room
(dark at first and now full of the lingering

spring evenings) 'good night.'
Presumably death is where time stops
so an afterlife might see past and present locked
in the same room. I ache to see you again

but what will we do with our selves
and the rest of our loved ones floating in the ether?
Beam eternal love at each other
while the cosmos falls apart and flickers out?

From here, it seems rather more likely that what-
ever-we-wish-to-call-it
will spare us all that. No matter. Drop
the odd hint if you can — a song, a smile

in a passing dream — and when I begin to die
fool me, be there waving furiously
door-framed inside that light-flooded
telescopic tunnel at the end

of the last fizzling neuron. See you then.

The Reverse

— *Cornelius Gijsbrechts, 1670*

Although his trompe l'oeil, 'The Reverse
of a Painting', is intended to deceive,
one double-take is all it takes to leave
the expected for the micro-universe:

nested rectangles, the frame's pale grain, the buff
canvas stretched and pinned with tiny tacks,
the price on a ticket fixed with sealing wax —
range-findings, star-charts, more than enough.

Beyond a trick then, his scrupulous look
at what is overlooked — details that wait
behind what hangs in MoMA or The Tate —
lifted the world of appearance off its hook,

turned it to the wall and then applied
equal pressure to the other side.

Lost Lens

i.m. Anthony Glavin

A new telephoto, somewhere in the gorse hills
above The Silver Tassie lounge-bar
and that bridge — beautiful

high, arched stonework (bullet-holed
from one of our wars). Clouds
blued into nightfall, rolled

over our desultory poking. Later, I told
my old friend (gone now
nine years) and I can still

see him, smiling, droll:
'Imagine, in a thousand years, someone
will find it and be able to infer

a whole culture.'

Evening Sun, Bullock Harbour

I could watch it for hours, this slight but definite

unstillness. Below the four by fours parked
amidst upturned rowboats where a grey cat prowls,
the tyre-draped wall's honey-coloured blocks

are aquiver with the reflected sea's
gently shifting transparencies, gauzy curtains
in a breeze-ruffled bathroom window,

a dressing and undressing of light.

Thigh Gap

Marked by the keen-eyed
who cull the tribe

of what is less
than desirable (presently, flesh),

you ache
for an absence, diamond-shaped

between your legs, hell
of Nothingness in a nutshell.

Nah, take a selfie
of your fuck-off grin, that selkie

you can never quite shed,
who'll tell you when you're being bled

of what you know — the truth:
Beauty is a brute.

Navels

A good thing to gaze at, your lover's
thimble of dark

•

See you at two, at the deep-shallow pool

•

Vestibule
for nothing more than the tip
of a finger or tongue, graze
of a stranger's guiltless eye

•

A mystery, the way yours is a magnet for fluff

•

Everyone to their own
free-floating punctuation

•

In the window of the tattoo parlour, a photo
of a sailor's encircled by boot-prints
and the words Navel Patrol

•

Forget the skewered eyebrow or chin,
the silver stitch in the lip,
the harpooned tongue —

here's the best place for sinking
that re-engagement ring

•

Stop looking at me there —
it tickles

•

Maybe to say: I exist —
like that bullseye
at the heart of the galaxy —
birth-story with a twist

•

Naba, nabel, navik,
pupak, pupek, pusat, puseg, pusod,

pito, piko, vico, ombelico, ombligo,
umbigo, umbilicus,

innie, outie — this
mammal-mark, shared scar

remembers

•

Vulture Bone Flute

— 38,000 BC

Fitting to see the oldest airs
salvaged from a raptor — the air
of its wing — and there is music

in our bodies, drums and strings,
wind instruments fulfilling themselves
so blood and sweat sings

to surfaces, half-blinding those eyes
lost in the swing of a scythe,
a notched sword, the haulage

of hominid arms through foliage —
music that runs like sap
back to the root

of our species jogging on the spot
wired to an iPhone — chants, field hollers,
deafening wars, silences — the body

bearing the mind away
with riffs, keys, tones, variations
on what's in us and what will come

to blow through our bones.

Hairpin

Afterwards, I kept finding them
lining the corners of cleared-out drawers.

I picked one up. It was blacker and glossier
than I remember.

Filings, a storm of magnetised particles,
unmagnetised, drift off like leaves.

Total eclipse: you can see the corona's
wild, ungovernable curls.

Cochlear Implant

'I could actually *hear* the skin
separating. I'd peel a hundred satsumas
just to hear that.' And immediately
I wanted to reach for one, dig my thumbs in
for the zesty, whispery rip —

as the inner ear uncoils its stethoscope
for the endangered ghost of a foghorn, tyres
on a wet road's unpeeling tape, the little whinny
a dog sometimes makes in its sleep:

shoes creaking into the fresh snow's crust
in the library of small sounds where satsumas
get peeled very slowly and Basho's frog goes *plop!*
cupped in that haiku, along with its pond
and summer's trembling meniscus.

New Poems

It Isn't Déjà Vu,

this peripheral swerve of windscreened light
burnishing a stand of firs against the slate
underside of a cloud,

a mountain's lit flank
revealing faint rills (famine scars?)
prodding a phantom

wound — not so much 'was
I here?' as the felt moment's swift
migration to molecules, its wingbeat

signature in the air

Rest On The Flight Into Egypt

— Rembrandt, The National Gallery of Ireland

The campfire in this nightfall
is roughly the size of a match
flaring in a dark corner,
the faces barely more
than fine-tipped dabs:

a shawled woman sitting
with a turbaned man who might
be a self portrait, a boy
kneeling, poking the flames,
(a cow breathing down his neck…).

Half-roofed by the canopy
of a squat old tree (a sturdy
oasis), they're grouped at the edge
of a pond or river, absorbed,
mirrored in the calm water.

Behind and above them
a shaft of clouded moonlight
sweeps from the left to pick out
a shadowy castle, crouched,
pin-slits of light in its watchtowers.

Whoa, easy there — time enough
for what comes: martyred walls
of shell-shocked cities, crushed
breathing spaces where all
that's left to play with is fire.

Here is a clearing, a bright seed
broad as an old tree, scale
we could live by — stretch of calm water,
animal-breath, firelight playing
on our faces — a detail.

Minoan Pendant

Yes — I press my nose
to the pleasantly warm glass —
it's a copy of one I saw
cased in the cool museum —
gold beaten to honey, a grainy
oval dollop, flanked by two
slim symmetrical bees —

garland for a civilisation's
rise and collapse, eye-dropped
five thousand years: a flash
of evening sun on a windscreen
or wing mirror — Heraklion's
scooter-life buzzing and humming —

as I step in to browse, become
mesmerized by the warm
dark eyes of the woman
who gives her spiel and moves
softly and with such grace,
that, after leaving, I hesitate

a moment on the pavement
then re-enter with a question
I know not to ask, but ask
anyway, to hear her voice
soften even more as she smiles
and shakes her hair — *no.*

Feathers

She gave me an etching she'd made
of a single feather, one of the short, curled ones
that plump ski-jackets and pillows. I asked

for it, though it may also have been a kind
of parting gift to something that could never
get off the ground.

                    *

Feathers found in amber
'represent distinct stages of feather evolution... from
single-filament protofeathers to structures
associated with modern diving birds.'

                    *

In an old copy of *The Rattle Bag* (bulked
with bookmarks: photos, letters, notes...) I found
a postcard I'd sent home from Perth in '74:

a picture of Highland Cattle, and taped on the back,
a grouse-feather, fresh as ever, blunt
as a shovel, its earth-brown speckles beautifully
covering the little I could find to say.

                    *

A microraptor — dark, small as a pigeon —
shed, along with its life,
colour, 'bundles of pigment' far
thinner than a hair, in stone

sensitive to tones: a touch
of oily iridescence,
shades of blackness in feathers:

ferns, broken bones, the crushed
umbrella light of the Cretaceous

opening for us.

Mobo

He told us he could 'smell'
when something had been composed on a screen:

these words, hunted and pecked
on a MacBook 5,1. Perfect

for drafting stuff on, but the next
will be more perfect, and the next

more perfect still
till technology

curls back to the body
as something so nano, so light, we can carry it

like a voice: Wordsworth
on his lake walks in his stride

composing *like a river murmuring and
talking to itself* — the body

electric ('carved out of a single block
of aircraft-grade aluminium')

warm on my lap — Times New Roman
more familiar than my own hand —

smell of words
before they drift downwind into language.

Dancing Plague

There's been a strange epidemic lately
Going amongst the folk

— Strasbourg, Alsace, 1518

O what is that sound which so thrills the ear

—W.H. Auden

Where, who was the music?

Frau Troffea was the first. She danced for four days,
the insides of her clogs slippy with blood.
A strange thing, and maybe it meant little,
unlike the last touches of The Great
Pestilence; unlike leprosy, famine, the pox
or that foreigner, The English Sweat.

Where, who was the music?

Other folk followed, at any time up to a score,
hopping, twisting, kicking up dust that danced
mingling with the dust raised by onlooking crowds,
amongst these, maybe, a few doomed to discover
how it feels to be hustled by your own body,
arrested, taken away.

Where, who was the music?

We did as we were ordered: schemes, edicts,
management of the afflicted: 'Flux in the blood'
might be danced out of the blood: guildhalls swept
into dancehalls, The Horse Fair displaced by a hammering
platform assembled quick as a scaffold: a stage
for proper music makers —

Where, who was the music?

trumpets, fifes — and hired dancers whose job
was to clasp the poor souls and spur them, spin them like tops
faster and faster, to out-dance, outquicken this thing
even as the old or weakened who couldn't keep up
stumbled, sagged, wilted and flickered out, gone
in some stranger's mechanical arms.

Where, who was the music?

No good. We did as we were ordered, searched
house to house, street to street, rounding up
wagonload after hopeless wagonload,
transported to the mountain shrine of Saint Vitus,
where strict monks set them to fasting, praying (even dancing
in red devotional dancing shoes)

Where, who was the music?

until something, it seemed, finally shifted. God
heaved off His curse. The shriven came clopping back
cured. Miracles. Or had this thing simply rolled on,
a thunder storm knocking the mountains? In its wake,
over two hundred graves, our faith shaken
as the unsteady, seasick earth.

Where, and *what* is the music?

The Ballad of Father Noise

When I saw the ghost of Molly Bloom
she wasn't on her own
but arm in arm through the Dublin gloom
with the ghost of Molly Malone

then a third one passed between them,
a man of the cloth no less,
and he raised a hand as if he meant
to say hello, or bless.

Did he help poor Peadar Clancy?
Was he at the GPO?
Did he hang out with the IRB?
No one can ever know

for Father Noise was born in brass;
two brothers dreamt him up,
a name on the bridge where crowds push past
children with paper cups.

Dublin has its passing souls,
its ghosts of flesh and blood,
the new maps laid across the old,
the Luas tracks in the mud,

and some names enter history
with a flash and a mighty roar
and some waft in like a summer breeze
and leave by the back door

but here's a name that should be sung,
a story yet to tell,
a rumour — test it on your tongue
until it rings a bell

and we raise a glass to his little plaque,
the storyteller's cause,
to the shadow man, the man in black
who *really* never was.

Elephant Place

The elephant housed in a wooden shed on Essex Street.

The elephant that belonged to a Mr Wilkins.

The elephant that in the early hours
of Friday 17th of June, 1681,
went up, with its tiny house, in flames.

The elephant that you could come and look at:
something extraordinary, a walking boulder,
its nose a tree, each little eye a knot.

The elephant you would have to pay to look at,
the fee too high for most.

The elephant whose immolation was a feast:
better than a hanging, rarer than a burning witch.

The elephant whose remains might offer something
tantalising: souvenirs, tradable relics.

The elephant cordoned off by a file of musketeers.

The elephant soon housed again by hammering
carpenters putting together its terminal shed.

The elephant whose extinction brought 'the eminent
Dublin physician', Dr Allen Mullen,
hurrying to make his proposition.

The elephant in need of surgical care:
delicate instruments to unclothe skin
and sinew, down to the very bones.

The elephant deserving skilled painters to make
'icons of each part.'

The elephant that by this time was emitting
'noisome steams' (and 'being very near
The Council-Chamber,' the Lord Lieutenant or Mayor
might declare a public nuisance
and everything be lost).

The elephant a team of butchers went to work on
'in order of the making of a skeleton.'

The elephant that was 'disjointed by candlelight.'

The elephant on whom Dr Mullen published
his famous paper, an account of 'the first
scientific dissection in Dublin.'

The elephant that became The Elephant Tavern
for over a century, until the sign
was taken down: a creaking, burned-out song.

The elephant that was never here, detained
in a foreign room that is a burning question.

The elephant, and what it holds in store.

The elephant whose white shadow was installed
in the Temple Bar Gallery.

The elephant that is breathing down my neck
a last trumpeted, ear-quaking, slaughterhouse roar.

Horse's Skull

for Michael and Beckie

On their coffee table,
weighty and tactile,

its wide forehead planing to where
nostrils would have flared.

The houses of life, death,
were exchanging guests

till the animal mind awoke,
tempted to stroke.

Notes On Dogs & Cats

Tree = wall
Tree = staircase

The tail is ever hopeful: metronome, propeller of delight.
The tail is a seismograph, warning, whipcrack of furious silence.

No matter how small, a dog has bulk and is earthed.
No matter how large, a cat treads one millimetre above the ground.

A dog is proof against intruders, wind in the chimney, ghosts.
A cat is partly an interloper, partly its own ghost.

A dog abandons itself to the chase; if it runs fast enough it will sprout
     wings.
A cat's wings are folded into the crouch, the stalk, the pounce.

A cat delicately sniffs the air, a leaf, a grass-blade…
A dog delicately sniffs the air, a leaf, a grass-blade… before being yanked,
snorting, to the centre of the earth.

A dog on its back = the ultimate submission.
A cat on its back = maybe.

Prufrock's predicament: He is a dog. She isn't.

In the wake of the dog: opportunistic campfires, tossed bones,
tradings of scent, the slow, painstaking deciphering of the human face.
In the wake of the cat: settlements, palaces, a niche for a household god.

A dog fills a space.
A cat opens one.

Frasp

It makes a sound halfway between someone saying 'Ah!' and the wind's vowel in the chimney.

It does not exactly scamper, nor crawl, nor exactly fly. It could be said, however, to hover.

You cannot feel its breath on your neck unless the house is utterly still, the wind turned off, the TV playing in a distant room (frasps are attracted to TVs but nervous of them).

It is translucent, though not invisible.

Like the pygmy shrew, it must eat continually to stay alive. Unlike the pygmy shrew, it eats in its sleep. Its diet is almost exclusively air, old skin/dust motes and the breaths of sleepers.

Depending on temperature, its skin changes in texture, from mouse-fur to lizard.

Only a handful of people have tamed a frasp. Once tamed, it will live happily up a sleeve, or a trouser-cuff.

It is *not* of the genus of ghosts.

The World

On a warm summer evening I pulled in to watch The World,
a 644 foot yacht docked
opposite the East Link toll.

Something to behold, its blockbuster title
up in lights, mounted near the funnel,
windows sacramentally purple, decks

girdled in white neon: self conscious as a poem
or stretch limo, nestling in its own
fragmented reflections, movie-ripples.

Other cars pulled in. A young couple paused to wave
and a boy in a Death Hammer t-shirt raised his hands
crabwise to take a snap.

Framed in a lower-deck window, a handful of slim
silhouettes regarded us. One pointed.
Their voices did not carry.

Ships in the night, ship in a bottle — soon
they'd be departing, heading back to the top
of their horizon's wall,

doing, perhaps, what the online brochure suggests:
'During the day you indulge in
a Balinese massage, sip a cup of coffee

in a neighbourhood café, or head to the marina
for a kayak ride on the open sea.
The same sea

that will inspire new ideas
as you look over
a business plan in your study.'

Hood Shots

You know the ones, where the viewer effectively squats
on the car bonnet, and the actor/driver has been told
to keep those hands busy or maybe just feels
it might look less static and more authentic

if the wheel keeps gently clocking back and forth,
back and forth — though anyone who has driven a car
can almost hear the wild, stock-car screeching
boofing other vehicles, skittling unlucky pedestrians —

but no, they just keep rolling, Old Man River
in a sushi-bar, as if the story were not in danger
of losing its grip, skidding out of its narrative groove
over the hard shoulder into that blank

where words and actions detach — But then who cares
apart from the odd lonely literalist who won't give
the film crew behind his eyes their well-earned
break, who refuses to realise what he has paid for:

to pass through that primordial, pop-corn-smelling foyer:
banks of upturned faces radiant as dials —
testings of suspension, tinkerings under the hood —
into the realm of shadows, masks, torch-light.

Nothing Is Stranger

than what we settle down with every night,
our bodies in the turned-on dark, its flight
into the swirling of the nowhere lights.

Nothing is stranger than what we truly own,
forgetting, when we can, that it's on loan;
nothing is stranger than our comfort zone.

Nothing is stranger than what wraps us up,
a butcher's parcel of flesh and bones and dream-stuff
out of which pokes the lover or the killer.

Nothing is stranger than our old familiar.

Phone Boxes

The last hangers on
are museum-temples, relics
from an age of privacy
that waited patiently in the rain

till yesterday; more and more
gutted over the years,
the good book torn
from its lectern, a lingering

benediction of old piss;
a perch, prop for
the unsteady, somewhere to slot
desperate invitations,

four-walled, breathless
confessions, a cube
of body heat misting the cold panes,
happy and unhappy

endings. Defunct, now
that privacy is unboxed;
now that — tucked, scrolled
in what trembles to hold

the entire whoomeroom — we wear
auras, hothousing plumes
of microwaves: each of us
a maker of speech

bubbles, a blower of glass.

The Next Best Thing

is the aroma-therapy candle in the bathroom at the end
of a car-burning estate,
the instinct to breathe in, suspend
judgement and keep the (above all lowercase) faith —

metaphysics of streetlights coming on
gradually, each flicker like an echoey cough,
pink at first as the rosy winter dawn
that will see them off —

finding we are each other's
strangers who stop in their tracks in the night
to stoop and kneel and murmur
to another: 'It's alright love, it's alright' —

The Mock Leaving, 1973

What can they make of me, so studiously dreamy
I fall asleep in strict Bill Tector's class —
my ear tuned to nothing much at all

unless it's the *sotto voce* lullaby
from the desk behind: Rooney
intoning the same Pink Floyd lines

over and over: 'the lunatic / is on the grass...'

Tube

Born in London but raised away, above-ground
in Dublin, the first time I entered you,
sinking through standing levels, brushed by that warm
intimate-exotic wind — smells of caked soot,
historical dust and the third rail's greased
lightning — I was home, buried, breathed on,
cradled and mortally coiled, lost and found.

The Elements

It's all
here: born buried
in earthlight, we open,
hum the song of the trilobite,
fall's flight.

*

Words are
mere air, Sappho?
Also embodied wind —
lungs blowing their warm front, stirring
her hair.

*

We're made
of it, tidal,
too full to not be spilt
emptying, though still managing
a wave.

*

Our eyes
rake the dark for
what forged and scattered us,
unsettled jarfuls of old light,
fireflies.

*

The fifth?
Dark, edgier
quintessence whose torn shapes
leave ragged holes in the song's net:
its gift.

How To Ask For A House In Poetry

I ask for a thatched and sheltered house,
truly clean and cleared
      — Old Irish legal tract

I ask for a house that keeps
its distance, though not too far
to shout goodnight at a neighbour;
a house with a smile on its face,
well-placed in the townland
while remaining on speaking terms
with trees, rooks and a badger — local colour.

I ask for a house keen-eyed
as a lookout, one that has climbed
beyond its topmost branches and listens
for the sake of listening, hears the tick
of branches on roof-tiles, the *phouff!*
of the boiler coming on, sees the wink
of headlights rounding a hill, can tell
the tread of a friend from that of the walking dead.

I ask for a house at home
with itself, so whether it's tucked
in the lee of a hill, overlooking
a road skirting the valley,
or a breeze-blocked yard jewelled
with smashed glass, it will rival
those gated drives and high kingdoms
whose passive windows rule the horizon.

I ask for a house wakeful
as the cat that also sleeps tight;
whose opening windows and doors
breathe like gills, easily exhaling the hard
feelings, a house that is ready
as any house can be for catastrophe and delight.

Notes

PAGE 48: THE GOLDEN GATE: CROSSING THE CHORD

From 'Jumpers' (Tad Friend's Letter From California, *The New Yorker*, October 13, 2003), about how the Golden Gate Bridge, since it opened in 1937, has become 'the world's leading suicide location', with at least twelve hundred victims. The quote is from Ken Baldwin, one of the very rare survivors. The 'chord' is the outermost, structural rim of the bridge, beyond the walkway.

*

PAGE 69: 'DON'T END WITH HISTORY OR THE SEA'

The poet is Kenneth Koch.

*

PAGE 112: FEATHERS

The quote, 'represent distinct stages of feather evolution,' is from an article by Hans Villarica, The Atlantic, Sept. 15, 2011.

*

PAGE 113: MOBO

Mobo is the abbreviation for motherboard.

*

PAGE 114: DANCING PLAGUE

There were a number of dancing plagues (or epidemics or manias) recorded in Europe between the 14th and 16th centuries. Both Pieter Bruegel and his son, Bruegel the Younger, depicted some of the victims, women unable to cease dancing. The epidemic in Strasburg in 1518 is investigated in some detail in John Waller's *A Time To Dance, A Time To Die* (Icon Books, 2008).

PAGE 127: THE MOCK LEAVING

The national Leaving Certificate exam (similar to the French Baccalaureate or the A levels in England) is taken in the summer at the end of secondary school in Ireland. The 'Mock Leaving' exam is held in schools earlier in the year as a taster or wake-up call for students.

*

PAGE 130: HOW TO ASK FOR A HOUSE IN POETRY

The following is the original Old Irish, from Gerard Murphy's introduction to *Early Irish Lyrics*

> Áiliu tech tuigthe téccartha
> n-urglan n-urscarta;
> ní ba tech cúan ná cethra,
> tech i mbí fíad is fáilte.
> Áiliu suide n-ard n-esartha
> i mbí clúm chubaid chosartha.

And here is Gerard Murphy's full English crib, part of which I took as a subtitle/starting point):

> I ask for a thatched and sheltered house, truly clean and cleared; let it not be a house for dogs or cattle, but a house in which there is honourable entertainment and welcome. I ask for a high strewn seat in which there is suitable well-spread down.

MARK GRANIER is a Dublin-based writer and photographer. His previous collections are *Haunt* (Salmon Poetry, 2015), *Fade Street* (Salt, 2010), *The Sky Road* (Salmon, 2007) and *Airborne* (Salmon, 2001). Prizes and awards include a number of Arts Council bursaries, The Vincent Buckley Poetry Prize and Patrick and Katherine Kavanagh Fellowships in 2011 and 2017.

His photographs have appeared in *The Guardian / Observer* magazine and have been exhibited in a number of group shows, including the Oxo Gallery in London, the Municipal Gallery in The Lexicon, Dún Laoghaire and the RHA annual exhibition. He has done cover work for various publishers, including Faber & Faber, Dedalus, The O'Brien Press and Salmon. *Irish Pages* featured a portfolio of his photographs in 2011.